# Leading Effective
# Bible Studies

A Practical Guide for

Transformational Small Groups

## Laura Krokos

Leading Effective Bible Studies

A Practical Guide for Transformational
Small Groups

© 2013 by Laura Krokos

www.MissionalWomen.com

How to lead an effective small group

# Contents

# Why Lead a Small Group?

When I went to college I got involved with a ministry whose focus was evangelism and discipleship. I was trained and encouraged to regularly go into the local high school and meet new people. I thought attending a basketball game would be a good way to befriend some high school freshman without freaking them out. I paid for a ticket to the game and entered the gym looking around for a group of girls to sit by, totally unaware of how much my life would be changed by this one decision.

I saw a group of girls and went to sit by one of them, her name was Candace. Candace was a freshman and we had small talk throughout the game. At the end of the game I asked Candace if her and her friends wanted to go out to lunch the next day. They said yes and I picked her and a handful of girls up the next day. That's when I met Cassie. Cassie and Candace, the girls God would use to radically transform my entire life.

My friendship began with this group of 12 girls. They ended up coming to camp with me where they all surrendered their life to Christ. When we returned from camp, the girls were eager to grow in their new relationship with the Lord and I began leading my first Bible study. Never having led a Bible study (or been in one) I was incompetent in myself but completely trusting the Lord had done a change in these girls hearts and He would continue to help them grow. I was confident He was able to use even me, the unskilled.

After talking to my Pastor and being given materials to use with them, the study began to grow. Both in numbers (to where there was soon 20+ girls and we had to split into two studies) and depth. I could see the Lord changing the girls from the inside out. I could see their desires changing; how they treated people, what they cared about and what they stood for. I was seeing the impossible happen right before my eyes; eternal change brought about by God in the hearts of His people, and He was using me to do it. Cassie and Candace and the other girls began to grow into strong disciples of Christ who the Lord used to minister to others. (Even to this day Cassie is a regional director for Young Life and some of the other girls are in full time ministry.) That was the defining moment of my life when I decided there was nothing else I wanted to do but to let God use me as He pleased in the hearts and lives of His people.

Since that first Bible study close to 20 years ago, I have led many many more. And it never ceases to amaze me how God uses Bible studies, a beautiful combination of His Word, His Spirit and the community of grace and truth to bring transformation. So why lead a small group? Oh let me count the ways!

*You get to partner with the God of the universe and see His life changing work in the lives of His people.

*You get to see God do the impossible (changing hearts) through a willing heart.

*You get to be a blessing to the Lord by serving others.

* You get to see spiritual multiplication set into motion that will continue for eternity.

* You get to see spiritual growth happen right before your eyes

* You get to start friendships that will continue into eternity.

* You get to see the Lord bless you and change your life at the same time.

* Experience a closer walk with Christ

* Experience an increased prayer life.

* See spiritual growth in your life and the people you're investing in.

* Grow in Biblical knowledge.

* Get to see the God of the universe use you to change the lives of others forever.

* Have a greater sense of personal discipline, faithfulness, and consistency.

* See your faith grow since being in a challenging position pushes you to trust God more.

* Grow in confidence of God's Will for your life .

* See God meet your needs. Matt.6:33

* See God grant you the "desires of your heart" Ps.37:3-6

* Experience the joy of standing before God, with thousands of people that you directly or indirectly helped into the Kingdom.

* Hear God, say to you, *"Well done good and faithful servant, enter into My joy!"* Matt.25:21

* Grow in courage.

* Experience God's Goodness poured out upon you. (Ps.31:19; 34:12; 84:11)

* Receive 100 times as much of what you have given up. - Mark 10:28-31

* Be part of a community where the word lonely doesn't exist, where a smiles replace suspicion and security replaces fear.

* And many, many more!

# So Who Does God Use?

You may be wondering, *"Can God really use me?"* or perhaps have even decided, *"I could never do that, I don't know enough"* Let me remind you that most of the people in Scripture were completely incapable.

So if being skilled and knowing all the answers isn't the qualifications for being a leader, what is? Let's look at three things we find in Scripture about what is needed in a leader. Let's call these the three 3 C's:

## 1. Godly Character –We all

know leaders whose ministries have been destroyed because of choice to choose sin. Sin is not to be taken lightly. Everyone who is still present on earth still sins, so it's not a matter of perfection but a matter of walking with the Lord in repentance. A righteous man falls seven times but rises again. (Prov. 24:16). A godly leader is someone who chooses to not live life by their own strength and ability but by the strength and empowerment of the Holy Spirit. Check out the video "How to Have the Fruit of the Spirit in your Life" at youtube.com/laurakrokos talking about how to practically live moment by moment dependent on the Lord. When we choose to let the Holy Spirit live through us the fruit of the Spirit will be what comes out of our mouths and lives; love, joy, peace, patience, kindness, goodness, faithfulness and self-control.

# 2. Compassion –The greatest

need of mankind is to love and be loved and often times love is communicated by the compassion we show people. Compassion is able to see an individual through the eyes of Christ. It is able to see their unique value and worth regardless of how they act. It is able to see where they are at and where the Lord wants them to be. It is having the attitude of Jesus, *"When he saw the crowds, he had compassion for them, because they were harassed and helpless, like sheep without a shepherd."* Matthew 9:36

Your love and concern speaks as loudly as anything you teach them. Giving, listening and caring for people in your group is one of the greatest privileges and responsibilities of leadership and is a key to the success of any group. 1 Thess. 2:7-12 is a great chunk of Scripture that gives example of the disciples and how they loved and served their disciples well.

> *"We were gentle among you, like a mother caring for her little children. We loved you so much that we were delighted to share with you not only the gospel of God but our lives as well, because you had become so dear to us. Surely you remember, brothers, our toil and hardship; we worked night and day in order not to be a burden to anyone while we preached the gospel of God to you. You are witnesses, and so is God, of how holy, righteous and blameless we were among you who believed. For you know that we dealt with each of you as a father deals with his own children, encouraging, comforting and urging you to live*

> *lives worthy of God, who calls you into his kingdom and glory."*
>
> *1 Thess. 2:7-12*

A compassionate leader is focused on the needs of the group members both real and felt needs; what pressures might they be facing, how to encourage them, how to communicate they are wanted as part of the group etc. It is having an attitude of being their willing servant, doing what's in their best interest.

> *"Be shepherds of God's flock that is under your care, serving as overseers--not because you must, but because you are willing, as God wants you to be; not greedy for money, but eager to serve; not lording it over those entrusted to you, but being examples to the flock." 1 Peter 5:2-4*

# 3. Commitment –All of us have

different personalities, life experiences, gifts, ways we think and unique relationship with the Lord. And all these things will play into how we lead others. But though we all will lead differently and uniquely beautiful, our commitment to the group will be what sets the bar. If you don't show up to your own group, expect that to be multiplied into your group members lives. The expectations and values you live out are going to be taken on by the whole group.

Commitment to the group members also means you have to put energy into planning. You need to pray for and think about your members development. What is their next step and how can you help them take it? What will help them walk with Jesus for a lifetime? I love how Paul describes the effort it takes to help people grow in their relationship with God.

> *"We proclaim him, admonishing and teaching everyone with all wisdom, so that we may present everyone perfect in Christ. To this end I labor, struggling with all his energy, which so powerfully works in me."*
> *Colossians 1:28-29*

I have provided in the back some practical tools to help you think through helping your disciples grow, so don't let this overwhelm you. And remember that we are not competent on our own but we have everything we need through Jesus Christ who strengthens us.

> *"Such confidence as this is ours through Christ before God. 5 Not that we are competent in ourselves to claim anything for ourselves, but our competence comes from God. 6 He has made us competent as ministers of a new covenant--not of the letter but of the Spirit; for the letter kills, but the Spirit gives life" 2 Corinthians 3:4-6*

# Count the Cost

In 2000 I went on a Missions trip to Nepal. The people are so hospitable and care for each other well. But planning ahead and counting the cost didn't seem like a big value of the culture. Almost every direction you looked there was a half-finished building. They began to build but ran out of money, so sat a building with metal beams and cement, completely unusable and worthless. Scripture talks about counting the cost before taking things on.

> *"Suppose one of you wants to build a tower. Will he not first sit down and estimate the cost to see if he has enough money to complete it? For if he lays the foundation and is not able to finish it, everyone who sees it will ridicule him, saying, 'This fellow began to build and was not able to finish.' "Or suppose a king is about to go to war against another king. Will he not first sit down and consider whether he is able with ten thousand men to oppose the one*

> *coming against him with twenty*
> *thousand?" Luke 14:28-31*

Leading a small group well requires counting the cost. So allow yourself time to process through the question, "What really will leading a group cost?"

**Here are some things to consider:**

# 1. Time- People in your group will not

grow overnight and neither will the relationships in the group. Henry Cloud says people grow emotionally and relationally when there are three elements. Grace, truth and time. When people experience that they are accepted no matter what at the same time we are honest with them and speak truth in love, over time they grow.

A good example of this a girl I discipled my first year on staff with Master Plan Ministries. My relationship with this girl did not start off super great. We got along ok, but because of her past experiences with Christians, she didn't trust me and it came out in disrespectful ways sometimes. Being my first year on staff I didn't have a lot of experience of how to win her trust or show her I cared for and loved her. So we would meet together week after week getting into the Word together. It wasn't awful, but it just didn't seem fruitful. I kept praying for her and one morning I felt very strongly that I needed to tell her something very specific I was struggling with. So I did. I pushed past the embarrassment and trusted the Lord would use my tiny step of faith. When I shared with her, she started crying and said, "that is exactly what I'm struggling with!" A deep bond was created and a friendship was born. To this day, this girl is one of the people I respect most in life and our relationship has only continued to grow.

If I had given up because it was hard, and not given our relationship time, I would have not seen God show off in such a beautiful way.

## 2. Energy - Loving and serving people

requires not only time but also energy. It means saying no to other good things in order to say yes to your group. I have lead a weekly Bible study for ministry leaders for eleven years. Saying yes to this group means

I have to say no to watching a favorite tv show, having friends over and being involved in things that would have been fun. But eternally investing in godly leaders is going to be way more valuable.

At times it can feel that people always want something from you and you may get tired of it. But reality is, that is our example of Jesus. We all want from Him.

> *"Let us not become weary in doing good, for at the proper time we will reap a harvest if we do not give up."*
> *Galatians 6:9*

# 3. Risk. Relationships are risky. There is

the risk of not knowing things, not being understood, having others disagree with you and the Bible, being seen differently than you'd like and on and on. You can also expect to face challenging situations: What if no one shows up, or only one person comes? What if someone dominates the discussion? What if some else took your bible study room?

Let me tell you another example from my first year of full time ministry. One of the girls in my small group Bible study, who I would meet with regularly sat down at the table for our weekly discipleship time and started yelling at me. I was stunned. I was having a hard time understanding what she was even upset about as she kept shouting untrue accusations at me. I had no idea where this was coming from and had no idea of how to respond. Let's just say that was one of my most discouraging days in ministry. I had given so much to her and in return she treated me like this.

When dealing with younger Christians, we need to remember they are not going to act like mature believers. They will do things and say things that hurt us. That's to be expected. The Lord uses fire to refine. It is risky to love and serve because there will be times you will not be loved well in return. But isn't that what Jesus did for us? He was hurt by the people He came to save and proved it was worth it in the end.

There is risk involved but there is also great reward. You will see people become Christians, others really grow spiritually, emotionally and relationally and the most exciting part is you will see God, the One

who spoke the universe into existence use
you to impact eternity!

You can also expect to grow personally in
your relationship with God. In fact you may
learn more than anyone. Learning to step
out in faith will change your life. You will
understand Scripture more as it is worked
out in your life and through the group.

# Starting the Bible Study

## Determine your Direction

Before starting a Bible study, you want to start with the end in mind. You want to think through your direction; Your purpose, mission, vision and roles. Your purpose defines why you exist as a group. Your mission defines what you want to accomplish. Your vision is a picture of the end result of accomplishing the mission and your roles are the things that need to happen to complete the mission and the people who are going to do them.

And the great thing is that the Lord has spelled the top two out for you. In Isa. 43:7, He told you the purpose He created you, for His glory. He also has given you a pretty awesome mission in this life, to make multiplying disciples (Matt.28:18-20, John 20:21) Well, that makes it a lot simpler for you. Now all you have to do is think about how.

Take some time to ask the Lord to lead your thinking and determine your direction:

**What is your purpose?** *To glorify God (know Him and make Him known)*

**What is your mission?** *To make multiplying disciples*

**What would it look like to accomplish the mission?**

**What roles need to exist?**

# Meet People

Now before a small group Bible exists you have to meet and invite people. Our tendency is to gravitate to a bigger group that's already meeting and invite people from there to our group. But really that is not most beneficial for anyone. Statistically, the 80/20 rule comes into play. 20% of the people do 80% of the work. So most likely the people who would come from that big group are the 20% that are already doing everything else. Ideally, you want to think of ways to meet new people and build a small group Bible study around them.

Meeting new people requires thinking and planning. You have to think about where, when and how you will meet people and then how you will invite them to your small group. When thinking through this, don't feel like you have to do it the way everybody else does. You have freedom to use your own unique experiences and gifts.

**Where will you meet people?**

**How will you meet people?**

**When?**

**How will you invite them to your Bible study?**

# Develop Relationships

In order to help the group grow from a brand new group to a strong, multiplying group, relationships need to be built and get strong. As relationships grow and deepen, you will have opportunities to encourage and challenge people to grow.

Suggestions for building relationships with the people in your group:

- Connect with them bi-weekly outside of your Bible study time. This can be a phone call, e-mail, text, Facebook or grabbing coffee or lunch.

- Pray for them and ask them specific things they'd like you to pray for them about. Then ask them how it's going with the things you are praying for them for.

- Give them specific things to pray for you. Be real and vulnerable. This is a good opportunity to show them maturity in Christ does not equal perfection.

- Ask how they are doing (relationally, physically, mentally, emotionally and spiritually) and offer encouragement and accountability.

- Observes them and provide regular affirmation.

- Seek to understand their personality, passion, and giftedness.

- Help them work through conflict whenever necessary.

Each new year of Bible study I lead with ministry leaders we do something called soul to soul. It is where each person gets 10-20 minutes (divide the time you have by the number of people in the group) to share their life story. Make sure it's communicated that things said in the group stay in the group and are not to be shared with others. Have the most vulnerable person go first to set the pace, have someone be the time keeper and encourage them to share about the events in their life that shaped them into the person they are today. This helps our group get bonded right from the start and gives us a foundation to build on.

# Serve them

Typically, people have two types of needs: real needs and felt needs. These categories are helpful, but not rigid. For example, people have needs to belong and be accepted. Usually, these are considered felt needs. People also have needs for a deeper relationship with God and forgiveness. Usually these are considered real needs. You will find it helpful to realize that people have needs they are aware of at the moment (felt needs) and other needs that perhaps they cannot identify. You will want to be tuned into both types of needs in the people you are leading.

# Planning the Study

Your first and second meeting most people are there to check-out the group. Their assessment will most likely be based on the perception of personal acceptance, not necessarily the content. Personal connection with the people will be the big thing that helps people feel like the weekly study is worth their time.

To help communicate that you value them as a person, I highly recommend you meet personally with everyone before or shortly after the first meeting. This will help you establish rapport and make a personal connection. It is also wise to meet with everyone personally within the first couple weeks to see how the new bible-study-member liked the group and to answer questions. This is the beginning of the critical relationship building phase.

To start the study, make sure everyone has been introduced in a nice way, maybe in a way that everyone can remember names and communicate the direction and tone of the Bible study. Usually it's a good idea for the leader to share their testimony so the group can understand better where they are coming from and to introduce a realness to knowing Christ. This will also help build your credibility in new people's eyes.

# Designing the best environment

You want to provide a safe place, that is free from distractions. It also helps to have it well-lit and a place where everyone can be on the same eye level. You can never go wrong with snacks and you might want to make sure you have a couple extra Bibles. It is also helps the connectedness of a group to have everyone on the same eye level. So try to find a room or place where everyone can be in a circle and on the same level.

You'll want to ask yourself:
**How can I help people feel comfortable?**
**How can I minimize distractions?**
**What conditions will enhance learning and discussion?**

# Creating A Sense Of Community:

If people in your group don't feel connected to you or the others in the group, chances are they won't come back. You are not in control of what people in your group think or feel or even how they act, but you can set a good example. When you respond to people graciously and look to meet people's needs, others will pick up on your attitude and being to imitate it. (You also can invite people in your group to do it with you.) Some things you can do to model a sense of community are:

- Regularly plan group time for members to share about their lives. (The Reveal Cards at MissionalWomen.com helps with this.)
- Maximize group interaction by preparing questions that will help the group interact with each other as well as God's Word.
- Help people to share what they are learning.

- Show concern for those in your group by asking for any needs that can be prayed for.
- Do something together as a group outside of the normal meeting time.
- Do activities with individual group members outside your group meeting.
- Pay attention when people are talking. Listen and try to understand by asking questions.
- Value other's opinions and steer clear from sharing pat answers.
- Be quick to laugh with them, share your struggles and victories. Be authentic and willing to open up and vulnerable.
- Tension in a group or among group members is inevitable. Agree to work through disagreements and conflict in a peaceful way.
- Observe your group members and how they interact with each other. You will learn a lot by watching and praying for them. *Are they comfortable talking about being a Christian? What do you observe about their relationships with*

*Christians and non-Christians?
How do they interact with others?
Are they shy, outgoing, overbearing,
controlling? Are they involved in
church or a Christian group? What
can you observe about their walk
with the Lord? Do they seem
hesitant to be involved in a small
group and if so why? What kind of
Bible do they bring? Does it look
like it's ever been used?*

Asking questions in the group will help the group to begin to connect with each other on a deeper level. And when they start feeling more relationally connected to each other they will be able to give and receive each other real encouragement and exhortation from God's Word. If you are talking the whole time and the other people have very little time to share their life and thoughts, they will not feel connected or feel ownership and will likely not be coming long.

Here's some questions you can use.

# Connection Questions

- What are you looking forward to in this study?
- What do you hope to get out of this study?
- How has God been drawing/pursuing you recently?
- What is a current longing?
- What do you think about most during the day?
- What causes you to feel discouraged?
- Describe your relationship with God right now
- How have you seen God use you recently?
- What is a strength you've seen God use to help others? Weakness?
- How do you experience the Holy Spirit in your life?
- How confident are you in your calling? Why?
- What are 3 things you value?

- Tell about a time God revealed Himself to you in a way that really affected you.
- What keeps you from believing what God says is true about you?
- How would your life be different if you had no fear?
- Describe a time when God asked you to do something and you didn't.
- Describe a time when God asked you to do something and you did.
- What is something you are looking forward to in heaven?
- What is one area that you battle shame or doubt?
- Describe a time the Lord comforted you.
- In what ways do you try to control your life?
- What is holding you back from living for the Lord the way you'd like to?
- What do you dream your legacy would be?
- What is a funny witnessing experience you've seen or had?
- What is a characteristic of God that's been meaningful to you?

- Tell us about a recent struggle or victory.
- What is a passage God has used in your life?
- What is one word to describe your day?

And here's some activities to help your group connect.

# Connection Ideas

## Highs and Lows

Have each person share their best and worst moments from the previous week.

## Uniquely Made

Go around the room and have each person share something that makes them different from anyone in the group. Something no one else in the group knows about them.

## Two Truths and a Lie

Have each person make three statements about themselves: two true statements and one lie.  For example: "I've never broken a bone.  I have 5 sisters. I was born in Nepal." The group tries to guess which statement is a lie.

## Personal Scavenger Hunt

Take 5 minutes and find the following items in your wallet or purse: Something that:
*you've had a long time
*you're proud of
*reveals a lot about you
*reminds you of a fun time
*concerns or worries you
Have each person pick a few to share with the group.

## Get To Know You Questions

*What do you do for fun?
*What would be your ideal vacation?
*What is the most memorable activity you did with your family as a child?

*What quality do you appreciate most in a friend?

*What is one characteristic you received from your parents that you want to keep, and one you wish you could change?

*What is a good thing happening in your life right now?  What makes it good?

*If you knew you couldn't fail and money was no object, what would you like to do in the next five years?

*What would you like said at our funeral?

*When, if ever, did God become more than a word to you, and how did it happen?

**Did You Know?**

This is great for a group that doesn't know each other well.  Find interesting facts about individual group members before the group meets.  Try to discover information that sets each person apart from the others, such as "I have a tugboat named after me" or "I once wrecked the same quarter panel of my car four times" or, "I have a twin."

Then make a sheet with one fact from each person and a blank beside this fact. Give everyone in the group a sheet and five to seven minutes to find who goes in each blank. When they find the right person they must also learn one other fact about that person. At the end, introduce everyone in the group in the order on the list.

## Life Maps

Thinking back as far as you can, draw a line graph to represent your life.

Consider the high points, the low points, moments of inspiration, moments of despair, leveling off times, and where you are now. The line will probably be a mixture of straight, slanted, jagged and curved lines. After you've drawn it, share what it means to you with the group.

## Write the Questions

Give each person a 3X5 card. You pick the topic and let them write the questions. For example, you choose "friendship" as a topic, and they each write out a question for anyone in the group to answer about friendship. For example, "What do you value most in a friend?" or, "Who was your best friend growing up and why?"

Then pile all the cards face down in the middle of the group and let people draw.

Topic ideas: jobs, life goals, funny stories, hobbies, family, fears, dating issues, significant relationships, relationship with God, etc.

**Heros**

Ask each member to name three people, past or present, they admire. Why? Or, ask them if they could interview anyone in history, who would that be and why? What one or two questions would you want to ask?

**Picture Time**

Draw and explain a picture of your day.

**Hot Seat**

Give each person (maybe one person a week) a chance to be in the hot seat. The other people in the group spend 5 min. asking them any question they want. The goal is for the person to answer all the questions.

# Planning the Bible Study

## Elements of a Good Bible Study

Since your mission, given by Jesus Himself is to make multiplying disciples, a good Bible study is not just people getting together or even a group of people getting together and studying the Bible. If you're really going to be about the mission the Lord gave you, your group is going to need 6 crucial elements.

# Crucial Elements of a Good Bible Study Group:

**1. Biblical Content.** The Bible is the inspired and inherent Word of God. It is shaper than any double edged sword piercing to the division of joints and marrow. God's Word through His Spirit brings about radical life change by those who spend time in it. Studying books is not bad, but Bible studies where a book of the

Bible is being studied is the absolute best. You can find many journals for each book of the Bible with questions to help you study and apply what you read can be found at the MissionalWomen.com store.

It is also extremely helpful when the group members aren't told what to think and believe, but have to figure it out on their own. It is important for spiritual growth for people to discover Biblical truth for themselves. The goal of a leader is to facilitate a good discussion on a passage in the Word and ask questions to help people discover biblical truth through observing, interacting, studying and processing the content together.

**2. Prayer**. Praying for each other, their immediate spheres of influence and the world keep the vision before the group. Using Scripture to pray is also helpful. There are free printable "Verses to Pray" at MissionalWomen.com as well as Connect Cards at the store that provides weekly things to pray for to keep you from getting in a request rut.

**3. Connection.** The group needs to become a team, committed to each other's wellbeing and growth. This will happen as you give time for people to feel known by giving them time to share how they are doing each week.

**4. Vision.** Vision leaks so you need to give a little bit of time each week toward casting vision of what life for the Christian is really all about-knowing Him and making Him known. Reading short excerpts from books like Radical, It's Not About Me, The Unexpected Adventure, Master Plan of Evangelism are good ways to do this.

**5. Training**. Many times there are things talked about that the Christian "should do" but they are not ever taught how. Each week there needs to be some time devoted to training on the things the Lord told us to do in His Word. Some examples are sharing the gospel, forgiving people, spending daily time with the Lord Etc. The Connect Cards are designed to bring Great Commission training element to Bible studies in at 10-15-minute chunk. Check them out at the MissionalWomen.com store.

**6. Outward Impact.** In order to not become a stale group, people need a place for applying what they are learning. The group needs to turn the focus from getting to giving. The goal is to help your group apply what is being learned through the power of the Holy Spirit. You could even brainstorm as a group how you act on the things you've learned that week and then talk about how it went the following week. The goal of a Bible study is not merely gathering information but is putting what is talked about and learned into practice.

Here is an example of what these elements could look like in a schedule.

# Example Schedule

### Vision (5-10 minutes)

Communicate God's purpose for the world and how we fit in the picture. Communicating about God's heart for people around the world and how He can use imperfect people to accomplish His eternal purposes is motivating. We exit to glorify God and be used by Him. When people really get that, they are moved to action away from theory, debate or platitudes.

Here are some suggestions for casting vision:

1. Highlight sections from a visionary book or magazine like:
- The Finishers by Roger Hershey
- Radical by David Platt
- It's Not About Me by Max Lucado
- Crazy Love by Francis Chan
- Master Plan of Evangelism
- Disciples Are Made Not Born

- Use the Operation World prayer book and a map to show what God's doing around the world.
- Articles from MissionalWomen.com, TheGospelCoalition.com or VergeNetwork.org

2. Share stories of how God is working in people's lives. Either share stories of how you've seen God show off in your life or those around you.

3. Visionary videos of what God is doing all around the world. (You can find some on youtube)

**Training (20 min.)**
Share practical, helpful, specific things about how to live and minister to others. Things like, how to have a quiet time, how to study the Bible, how to share Christ comfortably with a friend or stranger, how to answer someone's questions about Christianity, how to communicate through conflict effectively, how to share your testimony in three minutes, how to help a new believer grow, etc.

Help your group members develop the skills they need to effectively address situations like these:
*Using a gospel tract like the Knowing God Personally booklet.
*Communicating the role of the Holy Spirit (See the Spirit-filled Life videos at youtube.com/laurakrokos
*Demonstrating way of life evangelism
*Following up new believers
*Sharing personal testimonies
*Using evangelistic tools and apologetics
*Leading a small group
*Explaining how to know God's will for your life (Great resource at MissionalWomen.com)

### Prayer (10 minutes)

Prayer is an expression of our dependence upon God. Most small groups have time set aside for prayer, but often it's quick sharing of requests for the week without praying or it dominates the entire time. Creativity is the element most needed in prayer. Feel free to mix it up each week. Sometimes you need to ask, *"How has God answered prayer this week? What are you trusting Him for?"*

Another week you can hand out 3x5 cards and have people write their requests on the cards and then pass it to the person on their right and take it home to pray for that person throughout the week.

Try to remember to give the group time to share answered prayers so the whole group can be encouraged.

It's also important to pray for other people, issues and events outside your small group. Here are some other things to consider for prayer:

*Application of the vision time.
*Application of the Bible Study topic.
*Up-coming events.
*Personal ministry development
*Laborers for the harvest
*Ministry leaders.
*Government officials
*Different countries

## Bible Study (30 minutes)

Access the needs of your group and choose your content based on your group not on what you want to teach. Does your group consist of non-Christians, new Christians, older Christians that are non-active, fired-up

Christians or very mature Christians? It will also help to list felt and real needs you see. To help you find out where someone is at, don't assume, instead ask questions. Ask questions that would should you how well they understand the basics of living the Christian life and questions on how strong their faith is through their prayers and what they have done for Christ. After you have determined the needs of your group, then look for a study that will meet the real and felt needs. You can find some good studies on my site MissionalWomen.com as well as at LifeWay.

**Connect/Fellowship (time will vary)**
Your goal is to use this time to build relationships. Set the pace by being open and vulnerable and sharing what God is doing in your life and encouraging others to as well. You'll also need to do fun things together outside the meeting. Use the connection questions and connection activities above.

**Planning (10 minutes)**

Fit the announcements, delegation and business stuff of the meeting in this category. You'll need more or less time for this depending on the time of year, upcoming events and other planning.

# Dealing with discussion problems.

Sometimes things happen in a group that make for a not super healthy group or kill the direction and outward impact. Here are the top nine issues from The Ultimate Road Trip that hinder a strong Bible study.

1. **Silence.** After the leader asks a question, it's like everyone has taken vow of silence. Here's what you can do:

- If the question was good (open question), relax. People need time to think. You can always follow up with, *" Does what I am asking make sense?"*
- If the questions wasn't good or just seemed to miss the point, ask one of the backup questions that you have prepared to rephrase the question.
- Whatever you do, don't fill the silence with preaching.
- Encourage them with your non-verbal communication. Maintain good eye contact, smile, be relaxed,

lean toward the person speaking, nod your head as you listen.
- Encourage them with your verbal feedback: compliment their answers, convey acceptance, don't judge.
- Call on individuals who look like they have something to say.

**2. A wrong answer.** If someone says something contrary to Scripture. It's important to show you're not judging or putting down the person yet if it's an essential issue, you don't want to let it slide. Here are some ideas of what you can do:
- Use discernment. Determine if it truly a wrong answer or just a perspective different from yours.
- Be gracious and gentle. Don't get flustered.
- Redirect the question to another individual or to the rest of the group saying something like, *"What do you think the Bible says about that?"*
- If it's an off-the-wall response, say something like, *"That's an interesting thought. How did you*

*come to that conclusion?" "What
verses do you find saying
that?"* Lead them to the truth gently.
- Exclude inappropriate answers when
  you are summarizing.

**3. A Difficult Question:** Someone asks a
theological questions that would be hard for
anyone to answer.

- Admit that you do not have a good
  answer, but that you will try to find
  answer by the next meeting. The go
  ask someone that has a lot more
  Biblical understanding and study the
  question.
- Ask them why or what they want to
  know. It may not even be important
  to them.
- See if they would be willing to
  research the question and get an
  answer for the group.

**4. Not Being Able to Finish the Lesson.** If
you're not getting through all the elements
you desire, evaluate why.

- Did you start on time or did you start 15 minutes late?
- If the basic problem is that they like to talk and share too much at the beginning of the group: set some guidelines. Be careful with ice-breakers going too long.
- Are you spending too much time on one element so you're not getting to the others? Put that element at the end of the group time so it won't dominate the other elements.
- If the problem is spending too long on each question, try to pace yourself. Determine the time for each question, then move on to the next question. If you just cannot finish because the quality of the discussion is really good, just pick it back up next time.

**5. The non-stop talker.** If you let this continue it will hurt the community of the group. If one person is dominating the group here are some ideas.

- Direct questions to other members of the group.

- Set next to the talkative person and minimize eye contact.
- Ask for the talker's help in drawing out the quiet members.
- Ask them to keep his comments to a minimum.

**6. The Silent Person.** If you have someone come every week and not open their mouth and share their thoughts here are some ideas of how as to draw them out.

- Ask direct but low-risk questions that a shy person could answer comfortably.
- Sit where you can maintain good eye contact with those who seem reluctant to speak out.
- Give positive feedback when the shy person does respond to encourage further responsiveness.
- 

**7. Going off on tangents.** Rabbit trails are not always bad, but can be discouraging for the task driven people. It's important to keep it balanced and not let rabbit trails dominate the night.

- Try to be diplomatic and reflect an accepting attitude.
- Use a good question to get back on track.

**8. Disagreement and conflict.** It is ok to have disagreement and sometimes it can even be good to see if people don't agree but still choose to love each other well. However it can be nerve wracking when there is disagreement so here's some ideas of how to handle it.

- Do not let disagreements rattle you. Often then aid in learning.
- If two people disagree on a certain point, it may be profitable to talk about the two opinions.
- However, if also may be better to not let the disagreement become a tangent; and it would be better to pull the discussion back to the main point of the lesson.
- If two group members like to argue regularly, it would be a good idea to talk to each of them about being a distraction. Remember, problems

just won't go away, usually they get worse.

**9. The leader answering all the questions.**
When the leader answers all the questions, the group members can easily feel like they are not respected or valued. It also removes from them the opportunity to be a self-discovered learner. Here's some tips to help you from answering all the questions.

- Direct another question to a specific person in the group.
- Reverse the question back to the person who asked it.
- Relay the question back to the whole group?

# Facilitating Life Change- Going from Knowledge to Reality

Remember your direction; your purpose, mission and vision. The goal of the study is not just heaping up information, but to see God's Word and healthy community by the strength of the Holy Spirit change people from the inside out and make multiplying disciples. Life change will happen as people yield to the Holy Spirit's work in their life. Here are some things you can do to help foster a reliance upon the Lord and willingness to yield to the strength and ability of the Holy Spirit.

- **Model a heart that applies God's Word**. Never underestimate your modeling role as a group leader. If you are committed to solely to a fun group discussion, they will pick up on this attitude. Likewise, if they sense your commitment to applying

God's Word, they will be motivated to do the same. Be specific in sharing every week what you are learning and applying from the Bible.

- **Be committed to leading toward life-change**. Include application and life-change goals for your group. People need to see their lives change. Strive to address needs where the group can apply God's Word and see their lives change.

- **Structure your group time to encourage application**. Plan enough time in the study to talk about application. Begin each study asking about their application of last week's study. Give them an opportunity to share examples. Remember the goal of your small group time is discussion that leads to knowledge and application. If you miss the application, you miss it all.

- **Use Learning Activities.** Be creative, for example if you are studying loving your enemies, have group members do one kind act for someone they have difficulty loving.

# Multiplying the Group

As the group grows, you will need to break into two groups and as those groups grow, you'll need to break into two groups. But this beautiful multiplication which is the mark of a healthy outward focused group will never happen if you don't build leaders. From the start you'll want to be asking God to give you discernment to see who would be a great next leader for the group. When the Lord shows you, begin training that person by letting them plan, pray and lead with you. Give them little things and when they prove faithful with those, give them more and bigger responsibilities.

When your study is coming to the end, don't ask just one or two of the best and brightest; ask and invite all those who you see as potential leaders to join you and your leaders on mission with God. You could invite them to coffee and cast vision and encourage them with how you can see God using them to impact eternity with their willingness to serve Him. Specifically tell them what you see in them and what you have you observed about their life, their words, their relational skills, their gifts and talents, or their character. Explain what you see in them and how it could make an eternal difference in the lives of others. Good, solid observation about how someone is gifted by God can be strategic in helping that person discover his or her role in the body of Christ. Be observant and then share your observations!

We are inviting people into a mission that is directed by God and changes people's eternity. Tell emerging leaders how God has worked in your life and spiritual journey through your involvement in ministry. Help them understand that they have an opportunity to grow as a Christ follower and make a missional impact through contributing on a team.

After casting vision and asking someone to help lead or start a new group it is helpful to place a time limit on the decision. Give the potential leader time to think and pray, and then tell them when and how you plan to follow up with them. If you say you will call in one week, do it. If the answer is yes, share very specific steps on what comes next and give them some immediate leadership tasks.

# Evaluate

Every couple weeks it's a good idea to evaluate your group in light of your overall direction and make changes. Here are some good questions to help you evaluate.

1. Are we beginning and ending on time?
2. Are we getting through the essential elements?
3. Is everyone participating?
4. Did I successfully quiet the talkative ones?
5. Did I successfully draw out the hesitant ones?
6. Did I redirect comments and questions to involve more people in the interaction? (Or did I dominate the discussion?)
7. Did the discussion flow naturally, or did it take too many rabbit trails?
8. Did I show acceptance to those with ideas I didn't agree with?
9. Were my questions specific, brief and clear?
10. Are people growing into strong disciples?
11. Are they trusting and walking with God during the week?

12. Am I providing opportunity for future leaders to help lead?

13. Did my questions provoke thought?

14. Did each group member feel free to contribute or question? (Or was there a threatening or unnecessarily tense atmosphere?)

15. Did I allow for silence and thought without feeling uneasy?

16. Did I allow the group to correct any obviously wrong conclusions?

17. Am I casting vision for living out the Great Commission on a regular basis?

18. Am I providing training needed in order to become a multiplying disciple?

19. Did I refrain from expressing an opinion or comment that someone else in the group could express?

20. Did I vary the methods of conducting the discussion occasionally?

21. Are the group members feeling connected to each other and to me?

22. Am I keeping the group properly motivated in this demanding study?

23. Do I follow through from previous sessions by asking them later specifically how the truths have been applied?

24. Am I praying for each group member?

25. Is there a growing openness and honesty amongst my team members?

26. Is this group study enriching the life of my team as a whole?
27. Was I adequately prepared?
28. Am I spending adequate time preparing?
29. Did I encourage them to share what they have learned?
30. Did I encourage them to share the applications they have discovered?

# Bible Study Planner

Your goal for your group this week: *(What you want them to know, feel and act on)*

**Connection Time** *(and review of application from previous week)* (20 min.)
My connection question or activity is:

**Vision** (5-10 min)
I will cast vision for living on mission by sharing:

**Training** (10 min)
I am going to provide training on:

I am going to provide training for this through:

**Bible Study** (45 min)
We will read:


Main points I want to make sure to talk about:


Ideas for application:


**Prayer** (15 min)
We will pray for each other by doing:

# About the Author

Laura, the creator and host of Missional Women is married and has six kids, two of whom are adopted. Laura and her husband have been missionaries since 2002 serving with Master Plan Ministries. Laura is the Director of Women's Ministry and has discipled over 150 women, led over 30 Bible studies and speaks many times a year. Laura is an author and creator of ministry tools and resources. You can find her books and resources at the Missional Women store and connect with her on facebook,twitter, pinterest, youtube and instagram.

Made in the USA
Columbia, SC
08 April 2019